Jesus – Way of Peace

Jesus – Way of Peace

The Christian Aid/Hodder Lent Book 2003

Edited by Paula Clifford

Hodder & Stoughton
LONDON SYDNEY AUCKLAND

Copyright © 2002 by Christian Aid

First published in Great Britain in 2002

10 9 8 7 6 5 4 3 2 1

British Library Cataloguing in Publication Data
A record for this book is available from the British Library

ISBN 0 340 78717 1

Typeset by Avon Dataset Ltd, Bidford-on-Avon, Warks

Printed and bound in Great Britain by
Clays Ltd, St Ives plc

Hodder & Stoughton Ltd
A Division of Hodder Headline
338 Euston Road
London NW1 3BH
www.madaboutbooks.com

Contents

Contributors

Paula Clifford is writer and publications manager for Christian Aid in London, and a Church of England Lay Reader in the Oxford Diocese. She has published books on a wide range of topics and is currently working on a biography of Catherine of Siena.

Robin Eames is the Anglican Archbishop of Armagh and Primate of All Ireland (since 1986).

Andrew Goddard is Tutor in Christian Ethics at Wycliffe Hall, Oxford, and writer and tutor for the Bible and Politics module on the Politics and Theology distance learning programme at Sarum College, Salisbury. He lives in Oxford with his wife Lis and their two children.

Ramani Leathard is Senior Communications Officer in the Asia team at Christian Aid. She is a Sri Lankan and a communicant member of the Church of England. Currently a council member of USPG and a trustee of the Church of Ceylon Association, her areas of experience in development include Asia and the Middle East.

Bernardino Mandlate is a former bishop of the Methodist Church of Southern Africa in Mozambique and a former president of the Christian Council of Mozambique. He is currently serving with the British Methodist Church in Kensal Rise and Gospel Oak under the World Church in Britain partnership programme.

David Pain is head of Christian Aid's Churches team. With a background in adult religious education and community development, he has a particular interest in the processes through which Christians engage in social and political change. He attends the Quaker meeting in Oxford.

Helen Steven is the founder and director of the Scottish Centre for Nonviolence based in Dunblane. Born and educated in Glasgow, she worked as a volunteer in a Quaker programme in Vietnam during the war, and in 1979 was employed as Justice and Peace Worker for the Iona Community, of which she is a member.

Rowan Williams is the new Archbishop of Canterbury. Prior to this appointment Rowan, who was born in South Wales, had been the Archbishop of Wales since 1999. He has wide ranging interests in Christian theology and spirituality, was elected a Fellow of the British Academy in 1990 and is Chairman of the Trialogue Conference, which brings together professionals from the worlds of spirituality, psychotherapy and literature. He is particularly interested in the relationship between Christianity and the arts.

Introduction

Peace and reconciliation is a theme which is prominent in the pages of Scripture. The Old Testament promise of a Messiah who will be called 'Wonderful Counsellor, Mighty God, Everlasting Father, Prince of Peace' (Isaiah 9:6), which is fulfilled in the coming of Jesus who offered his followers a peace such as the world cannot give (John 14:27), is dear to Christians the world over.

Yet we live in a world that is marred by conflict of all kinds – between individuals and groups, between religions and nations. The causes of conflict are many and varied but the effects across the world are all too familiar, with people being driven from their homes, subject to poverty, hardship and sickness, and governments devoting more and more of their resources to military use. Conflict and peacebuilding are urgent practical issues for many thousands of people, as well as matters of concern to everyone who cares about the future of God's world and his people.

The daily readings for this year's Lent book are taken from either Isaiah or the Gospel of John. They provide a challenging basis for reflection, and are intended to help us think more deeply and pray more knowledgeably about some of the issues involved.

I am grateful to the distinguished contributors to this book for taking time out of their busy lives to bring to it the fruits of their experience of conflict and peace. They include Archbishop Robin Eames, who has worked in Northern Ireland during some of that community's most troubled years, and Bernardino Mandlate, whose church was instrumental in bringing about an end to the war in Mozambique. There are reflections on theological aspects of peace and reconciliation and on the effect of conflict on the lives of ordinary people. As we move through Lent to Passiontide and Easter, may we find here opportunities to explore the biblical texts and to reflect with added insight on their meaning for our world today.

Paula Clifford

Using this book in small groups

Jesus – Way of Peace can be used as a Lent book by small groups meeting on a weekly basis as well as by individuals using it for private meditation. One way of doing this is to take one of the passages for the week as a focus for discussion and prayer. Group members should be encouraged to use the book each day at home as well, so that they can also bring their personal reflections on the other passages to the group meeting.

The following outline assumes that groups are meeting weekly, beginning in the week of Ash Wednesday. There is no study suggested for Holy Week, when group members may wish to attend special services instead. Group leaders will probably need to examine the passages suggested with the help of a biblical commentary in order to help the group with the context and with questions of interpretation. The questions suggested for discussion may be modified or developed to fit the interests of the group; in each session there should be a significant amount of time set aside for prayer.

Session 1: The promise of God's kingdom of peace

Isaiah 5:1–10: Looking for justice

Theme:
God's vineyard

Questions for group discussion:
1 Reflect on the parable of the tenants (Luke 20:9–15): what light does this throw on the Isaiah passage, and vice versa?
2 How do you understand peace in the light of this passage?
3 What forms of justice are needed for people to enjoy lasting peace?

4   What importance should we attach to retribution?

Add any further reflections from the other passages set for this week.

Some suggested prayer topics:
Pray especially for people who are adjusting to peace after war; ask for forgiveness for injustice past and present; and pray for an end to particular forms of injustice identified by the group.

Each week pray for a specific area of the world where there is conflict.

Session 2: The revolution of Jesus

John 8:1–11: Compassion and forgiveness

Theme:
Non-violent action

Questions for group discussion:
1   In what ways is Jesus' teaching here 'revolutionary'?
2   Is it possible to show compassion without taking some kind of action?
3   In what circumstances is civil disobedience justified? When is it not?

Some suggested prayer topics:
Pray for prisoners of conscience in different parts of the world; pray for those whose compassion leads them into dangerous situations; and pray that Christians who have been wronged may be quick to forgive their accusers.

Session 3: Religious conflict

Isaiah 58:1–9: The pride of self

Theme:
Religious rivalry

Questions for group discussion:
1   What in particular arouses God's anger in these verses?
2   Is there a place for the discipline of fasting for Christians today?
3   What forms of worship or religious practice are we particularly attached to? How can we avoid the risk of taking a self-right-eous pride in them?
4   What experience have you had either of conflict between people of different religions or of people of different faiths living peacefully together? What have you learned from this?

Some suggested prayer topics:
Pray especially for Northern Ireland and the peace process, pray for Christians there who long to live peacefully together; pray for peace within communities where different religions are repre-sented, and for peace between nations divided by religion.

Session 4: Conflict between nations

Isaiah 37:15–20, 33–38: An answer to prayer

Theme:
Praying for peace

Questions for group discussion:
1   How should we pray for nations at war?
2   What kind of peace should we be praying for?
3   In what ways today might 'all kingdoms on earth know that you alone, O Lord, are God' (Isaiah 37:20)? (Pray that these things might come about.)

Some suggested prayer topics:
Give thanks for the role of the churches in bringing about peace in Mozambique and pray that the Church may be effective in other areas where there is conflict; pray that those who live in peace may be faithful in praying for those who do not.

Session 5: War and peace at the end of the age

Isaiah 25:1–12: Joy for all people

Theme:
A new community

Questions for group discussion:
1   What are the distinctive features of the people who belong to the new community portrayed here?
2   How does this passage compare with Revelation 21:1–4?
3   In what ways do today's modern cities oppress those in need? What can be done about it?
4   What is the role of Christians who live in 'cities of ruthless nations'?

Some suggested prayer topics:
Pray for our cities, for the people who live, work and worship in them; pray for those who can see a future only in terms of

destroying others; pray for those who long for the Lord to wipe the tears from their faces and ask that Christians may be faithful in focusing on the biblical vision of joy to come.

Session 6: Discord and harmony between individuals

John 15:12–17: The greatest love

Theme:
The sacrifice of the cross

Questions for group discussion:
1 Ask the group for examples of people like Karuna who have given their lives for others. What can we learn from them?
2 What groups of people (as opposed to whole nations) do we see as a threat to a peaceful way of life? How can the example of Jesus' love help us to resolve our conflict with them?
3 What do Christians have to offer to political peacemaking processes?

Some suggested prayer topics:
Give thanks for the sacrifice of Jesus on the cross and for his promise of new life; and give thanks for people, unknown outside their own communities, who have followed his command to give their lives for others; pray for a fresh awareness this Passiontide of the suffering of Jesus and the depth of his love.

Either in the final session or on a separate occasion, discuss what the group has learned about conflict and reconciliation and about praying for peace. How can you use this learning once Lent is over?

Jesus – Way of Peace

INTRODUCTION:
THE PROMISE OF GOD'S KINGDOM OF PEACE

PAULA CLIFFORD

Swords into ploughshares
Isaiah 2:5

Come . . . let us walk in the light of the Lord. (Isaiah 2:5)

Throughout Jesus' ministry, beginning with his time of temptation in the desert, there was conflict. Jesus experienced internal conflict, with the forces of evil, and external conflict, with powerful political and religious leaders as well as with ordinary people who could not understand what he was about. For him that conflict ended at Calvary. And with his resurrection to new life began a new era in which human sin and conflict is subject to the transforming power of the cross. It's a progression which we can see too in the book of Isaiah, which reflects very real conflicts between nations and between people and God, yet also looks forward to the Day of the Lord, a time when such struggles will be replaced by a new era of peace.

Several generations of people in the UK have little or no experience of all-out war. But the memory of past wars remains very much alive. Families remember how at the outbreak of World War II young children were sent away from big cities to the alien environment of the countryside or to places on the other side of the world. Young men were wrenched away from their homes; women took on new work and new responsibilities. Even before the killing started, people's lives were turned upside down.

The prophet Joel encapsulated this upheaval in an agricultural image: 'Beat your ploughshares into swords and your pruning hooks into spears' (Joel 3:10). Isaiah takes the same idea but turns it the other way round to show that peace is as big an upheaval as war, when people will beat their swords into ploughshares and spears into pruning hooks. True peace – which, says the prophet, can only come about when God is universally recognised – means not simply putting one's weapons aside but transforming them, turning them to a completely different use.

A recent art exhibition, called 'Swords into ploughshares', illustrated exactly that. Artists from Mozambique took weapons used in the war that had devastated their country and turned them into sculptures, transforming them, giving them new life.

This is the process we shall have in mind throughout our journey through Lent to Good Friday and Easter Day, a journey of transformation as we reflect on the upheavals of conflict and the revolution of peace.

Lord, as we begin this season of Lent, may we walk each day in your light; remove our complacency, open our eyes to the conflicts in our world, and show us your way of peace.

Day 2

Disaster
Isaiah 3:9–15

What do you mean by crushing my people and grinding the faces of the poor? (Isaiah 3:15)

When a country's resources are poured into meeting the cost of war, it is the people who are least able to fend for themselves who come off worst, as money that might otherwise be spent on social services is diverted to military use. And the widespread destruction caused by modern warfare hits hardest those who can't afford to rebuild their homes or businesses.

Through his prophet, God condemns in no uncertain terms the elders and leaders of Judah who have inflicted immense suffering on the country's poorest people. Isaiah looks forward to the fall of Jerusalem and the conquest of Judah in 587 BC and the subsequent exile of the ruling classes in Babylon. That disaster is laid at the door of the leaders. But it's clear that this doesn't refer just to poor military leadership. The ruling class has been exploiting the people, taking away what little they possessed, and in such a situation defeat is perhaps inevitable. The people who have been so mistreated, to the extent of being totally crushed by their leaders, will have neither the will nor the strength to support them in times of danger. And so the people's suffering is compounded by the suffering of defeat.

When I visited Kinshasa, in the Democratic Republic of Congo, in 2002, I was hundreds of miles away from the war zone in the east of the country. Yet the effects of war could be seen everywhere. People were on edge, fights broke out at the slightest provocation, and the level of poverty in some areas was almost unimaginable. Perhaps worst of all, the government had no money left to care for the tens of thousands of people who were HIV-positive, and nothing to invest in education programmes to stop the virus spreading still more. In this war, the weakest people were being abandoned. Their health and education services were being plundered to pay for it.

Isaiah's message is that the way of peace is also the way of justice. We're reminded that Judah's leaders brought disaster on themselves through their reckless self-indulgence and their contempt for other people, God's people. The way out of that disaster could only be found through justice and reconciliation between the people themselves if they were also to be reconciled to God.

Lord God, bring relief to all your people who have been crushed by war. Give them wise and compassionate leaders who will take them forward in the ways of justice and of peace, so that out of national and personal disaster may come a new and lasting hope. Amen.

Day 3

Looking for justice
Isaiah 5:1–7

He looked for justice, but saw bloodshed; for righteousness,
but heard cries of distress. (Isaiah 5:7)

The Old Testament history of Israel is an often repeated saga of success and failure, the story of a people for whom God provides everything but who all too often fail to live up to his expectations. Their land is described in the most appealing way, 'a good and spacious land, a land flowing with milk and honey' (Exodus 3:8). And an equally attractive metaphor is used to describe the people themselves: they are God's vineyard – an image taken up by Jesus in the parable of the tenants (Luke 20:9–15).

God's vineyard has everything going for it: a conscientious owner, excellent location, the best vines and permanent buildings. But despite all these advantages, instead of the expected good crop there's only bad fruit – small sour grapes which cannot be used for anything. God's response is to destroy the whole thing by allowing the enemy to trample it into the ground. Only at the end of the parable do we learn what lies behind this. What God was looking for in his people was justice and righteousness. Instead they responded with bloodshed and cruelty.

This destruction may seem excessive, but it's an indication of how much God values justice and requires it from his people. Justice is what motivates his own actions in his care for his people. Using a different metaphor Ezekiel puts it like this: 'I will bind up the injured and strengthen the weak . . . I will shepherd the flock with justice' (Ezekiel 34:16).

Rwanda is a country which has similarly known disappointment and destruction on a vast scale. Originally rich and fertile, the demands of its large population led to famines in the late 1990s, just a few years after the genocide which killed hundreds of thousands of people. The judicial system is now very slowly bringing some of the 125,000 people accused of complicity to justice, and Rwandans are working at reconciliation and trying to make a living. Through Christian Aid's partner the Episcopal Church of Rwanda, in Kigeme I met an 11-year-old schoolgirl who was just beginning to get an income of her own from the animals she rears. Her name was Angelique Nyirahabimana – which means 'God will provide'.

Jesus said, 'I am the vine; you are the branches. If you remain in me and I in you, you can bear much fruit.' Lord Jesus, keep us abiding in you, that as co-workers with you in your vineyard we too may provide for your beloved children.

Day 4

Dreaming of peace
Isaiah 11:1–9

They will neither harm nor destroy
on all my holy mountain. (Isaiah 11:9)

Isaiah's vision of a future king and the return of a time of perfect peace follows an account of terrible destruction. In Isaiah 10 God has used the powerful Assyrians as a means of carrying out his judgment against his unjust people: 'I dispatch [the Assyrian] against a people who anger me, to seize loot and snatch plunder, and to trample them down like mud in the streets' (10:6), even though the Assyrians are also in line for God's punishment.

The horrors of this war that tramples people into the ground are offset by the picture of the new order in Isaiah 11. In place of unjust leaders comes one who has God's Spirit of wisdom, who 'delights in the fear of the Lord' (v. 3). Instead of oppression the people will experience righteous judgment. And this new reign of peace is not only for people but for the animal kingdom as well.

The idea of animals who are naturally antagonistic to each other co-existing peacefully may be contrary to the laws of nature, but it is a very effective way of presenting a way of life that is wholly free from danger. It also suggests that the new order of peace is characterised above all by respect for God's gift of life, whether human or animal.

I recently visited the South Asia Coalition on Child Servitude in India. This organisation rescues young children from working in factories and from other forms of labour, and offers them rehabilitation in safe children's homes (ashrams) before helping

8

them to get into school. I was very struck to find that in one of the ashrams the children were being encouraged to live alongside domestic animals, including a couple of very large dogs, and to respect them, something which is quite unusual in that culture. This was seen as an important step in enabling the children to move away from the hostility and ill-treatment they'd previously experienced to a new life which, if not idyllic, was at least one where they were at peace with themselves and with one another. As 12-year-old Deepak put it, 'Being here makes you very sociable. I have so many friends now' – a huge contrast with the exploitation and isolation that had previously marked his life.

> *You have been my refuge, a strong tower against the foe.*
> *I long to dwell in your tent for ever and take refuge in the shelter of your wings.*
> *For you have heard my vows, O God; you have given me the heritage of those who fear your name. (Psalm 61:3–4)*

Day 5

HELEN STEVEN

A lone voice
John 1:19–28

John replied in the words of Isaiah the prophet,
'I am the voice of one calling in the desert,
"Make straight the way for the Lord."' (John 1:23)

This is the starting point of revolution. The lone voice, the clear-eyed one, who suddenly sees that something is wrong, that all is not right with the world, and starts shouting about it, being difficult and troublesome, rocking the boat. Other people find it embarrassing, accuse you of being extreme, even mad, exaggerating, and sometimes you even have doubts yourself.

John the Baptist must have seemed all of these things. He delivered his message of radical justice in the most uncompromising way, haranguing his listeners as a 'brood of vipers', denouncing their way of life, and calling for repentance. Even his lifestyle was disturbing, a wild-eyed figure carrying the simple lifestyle to excess.

It is difficult to be different. I recall my embarrassment travelling into Glasgow on a Saturday morning with a coffin on the seat beside me. I was going to a demonstration, but all the time wishing with all my heart that I could just be a normal Saturday morning shopper.

John's message was a clarion call to justice, reflecting the vision of the prophets of a world where crookedness, inequality and injustice were made straight – 'the axe laid to the root of the trees' – and the way prepared for the coming of God's kingdom in Jesus. John never lived to see the completion of his revolutionary dreams.

Twenty years ago I took part in a Bible study led by a member of the Iona Community on the Jubilee message of Leviticus. He spoke of the cancellation of debt and linked it to the crushing 'debt' of the poor countries of the world. The idea had never occurred to us – we thought it impossible that government would ever listen. Twenty years on, the movement to drop the debt is one of the fastest growing campaigns in the country.

People flocked out into the desert to hear John the Baptist. The message of justice is still urgently compelling. The world's poorest people are still on tiptoe with expectation.

> *Lord, give us open eyes that we may see injustice, ears attuned to the quiet suffering of the oppressed, and hearts soft enough to break.*
> *Give us the strength to be different, to make fools of ourselves, and to stand out for justice, that we may be part of the preparations for your reign of love.*

Day 6

A holy rage
John 2:13–22

*To those who sold doves Jesus said, 'Get these out
of here! How dare you turn my Father's house
into a market!' (John 2:16)*

We don't often think of Jesus in a towering rage. Gentle Jesus, meek and mild, is much safer, more comfortable and comforting. But anger has been described as the other side of the coin of love. Jesus was burning with passion – 'zeal' is the word used. So what was it that had provoked this rage?

Jesus was going up to the Temple at the time of the Passover, that most precious time when Jewish people travelled long and weary miles to celebrate in all solemnity God's saving work of liberation in the Exodus. And Jesus found the forecourt of God's house being used as a marketplace to cheat and exploit the sincerity of the worshippers. It was an affront to the very core of religious belief.

His overturning of the tables was not a polite 'Excuse me while I tip over your tables'. A minister preaching on this text recently lifted a table above his head in front of the congregation and dashed it to the stone floor with a crash, shocking the congregation out of their seats. This was non-violent direct action of the most challenging kind.

South African Allan Boesak writes of a 'holy rage':

The ability to rage when justice lies prostrate on the streets and when the lie rages across the face of the earth. A holy anger about things that are wrong in the world. To rage against the ravaging of God's earth and the destruction of God's world. To rage when little children must die of hunger while the tables of the rich are sagging with food. To rage at the senseless killing of so many and against the madness of militarism. To rage at the lie that calls the threat of death and the strategy of destruction 'peace'.[1]

'You must not turn my Father's house into a market.' Is that not exactly what we are doing to the temple of God's earth, as we ravage and plunder its riches, exploit the poor for profit, and protect our interests with weapons of mass destruction? These things must surely anger us if we love God's world, and such anger must surely inspire us to action.

Three years ago a close friend of mine threw the entire contents of a laboratory used for the testing of equipment linked to the Trident nuclear submarines to the bottom of a Scottish loch. She told me that with each splash she felt a pure surge of liberation from slavery, injustice, oppression and nuclear death.

Martin Luther King said that non-violence exposes the underlying violence of society. It was when King began to challenge the Vietnam war and the scandal of inner-city poverty in the United States that he was assassinated. Jesus' actions turned the world upside down, so they plotted to kill him.

> Lord, anger is a powerful emotion. Help us not to destroy ourselves with its bitterness or feelings of helplessness and impotence. May we never use its strength to harm or destroy others, but always seek ways to use it creatively for good. May our anger always be guided by love.

Day 7

*Jesus told them, 'The right time for me
has not yet come.' (John 7:6)*

To testify is to bear witness to the truth. Early Quakers experienced religious conversion in terms of the 'Light Within'. In their encounter with the Light of Christ they spoke of the 'Desolation of the Light' in which the pure radiance of Christ revealed the extent and gravity of sin.

In his book *Rich Christians in an Age of Hunger*, Ron Sider speaks of 'corporate sin' – the ways in which all of us are inextricably bound up in the systemic violence of global injustice. It is not enough to seek personal salvation; our salvation is bound up with that of our hungry neighbours.

However, there is a contrast here in the ways in which Jesus is acting. Not the public blaze of exposure, but a quiet, almost furtive secrecy. Jesus knows full well that his life is in danger and that the net is closing in on him.

'The world hates me.' He is in the unenviable position of whistleblowers who publicly expose the wrongdoings and evils of society, and is faced with the difficult decision of working out whether to continue in the blaze of publicity or go underground for a while. We see here Jesus the wise strategist and careful activist: 'For me the right time has not yet come.' Here there is that delicate balance between openly challenging injustice, as in his actions in the Temple, and prudently waiting for the most appropriate time. A fine balance indeed. Not the inaction which promises to act when it is safe to do so, but the wisdom of waiting and discerning when it is right to act.

In 1972 during the Vietnam war I worked with Father Chan Tin, a priest who was sending information about torture to Amnesty International. He was under constant surveillance and he lived under house arrest in his church in downtown Saigon. This was where I would go to meet him to pass on vital information. Six years later, after the end of the war, with a change of government, I went to visit Father Chan Tin. He was still under house arrest, even under a new regime, still quietly witnessing to human rights abuses, keeping his head down amid threats to his life. A quiet courage hidden from the world.

Give us discernment, Lord. Help us to know when to hold back, when to continue working for your kingdom quietly without reward of recognition. Help us to be gentle with those who cannot publicly witness, and give us courage when we are called to make our own witness.

Day 8

Compassion and forgiveness
John 8:1–11

*'Neither do I condemn you', Jesus declared.
'Go now and leave your life of sin.' (John 8:11)*

It has become apparent to me over the years that Jesus in his actions consciously and deliberately broke the law, in public and symbolic acts of civil disobedience. He broke the Sabbath laws, kept company with the 'wrong' people, ignored the eating regulations, when he could easily have done otherwise, and as he approached Jerusalem these acts became increasingly high profile and challenging.

In this vivid picture of the unfortunate woman dragged before Jesus for judgment, a deliberate trap has been set by the religious authorities. The law specifically requires death by stoning. How could Jesus claim to be a rabbi and teacher of the law if he openly defied it?

His well-known turning of the tables is brilliant, and incidentally leaves us with the unanswered question: who and where was the man involved? Then, in the last part of the story, when he is alone with the terrified and humiliated woman, Jesus says, 'Neither do I condemn you.' Not only is this another challenging of authority in his claiming the right to forgive her, but it shows clearly the guiding principle behind his breaking of the law – compassion.

Without a Christ-like love of humanity and gentleness towards the frailty of our human condition, revolution, however just its cause, becomes a merciless, ruthless and dangerous tool.

Gandhi used to talk about 'pouring love into the institutions', and non-violent action is based on the premise that even the most faceless of political systems or corporations is made up of ordinary human beings with feelings and a capacity to change, with a spark of humanity or 'that of God', and that it is this potential that can change the world.

It is this compassion which forms the basis of all attempts at peacemaking and reconciliation. One of the most moving pictures to come out of the tragedy of 11 September was when a group of New Yorkers who had been bereaved by the attacks on the World Trade Center went to Afghanistan to meet women who had lost loved ones in the bombing. Where the world condemned, they were attempting to forgive.

Lord, it is so easy to take the moral high ground. Give us the humility and the understanding to see beyond other people's actions to the human reasons behind them. Help us to ask for forgiveness ourselves and to give it generously.

Day 9

Challenging the powers
John 11:38–53

*The Romans will come and take away both
our place and our nation. (John 11:48)*

In some ways the raising of Lazarus was the greatest symbolic act of civil disobedience of them all, and it immediately raises huge questions of authority. What gave Jesus the right to challenge what God ordains? Even in our own society, and certainly in the Jewish society of his day, death is surrounded by taboos and barriers. How dare he contravene not only the religious laws, but the very laws of nature themselves?

More than this. In the raising of Lazarus, Jesus challenged the very power of death itself. The threat of death is the ultimate sanction that can be exercised. If death itself no longer holds any terror, then there is no tyrant or system that has any control over us. The ultimate fear is at an end, and the chains that bind us are shattered.

A plaque marks the spot where Martin Luther King was shot, and it simply says, 'Don't let the dream die.' We ourselves may die, but the hope, the vision, the struggle, live on.

When the inspirational Chilean folk singer Victor Jarra was tortured to death after the overthrow of Allende it might have seemed the end of a dream for the people of Chile. Crowds at the funeral procession were covered by machine guns from the rooftops and the oppressors seemed to have won the day. Suddenly someone in the crowd shouted, 'Victor Jarra, *presente*,' and thousands called out, one by one, '*presente, presente*' – here with us.

In Chile, as in Jerusalem in Jesus' day, the fear of the authorities was of outside intervention by the 'great powers'. Will such spectacular defiance not bring down the might of the Roman occupier upon us? Will open demonstration not bring US intervention to protect the stability of the market? Keeping the country quiet is good for business and doesn't affect the profits.

When Archbishop Romero of El Salvador preached openly against the death squads, he knew he would be killed. But the grave itself had lost its power to control. The revolution of Jesus challenges the power of unjust rulers and of unjust corporations and offers an alternative way of justice. And in challenging and defeating the power of death, Jesus offers, in its place, life.

Lord, we give thanks for the great host of brave people whom death itself could not silence. May we do our part to keep their vision alive.

Day 10

Now is the time for judgment on this world;
now the prince of this world will be driven out. (John 12:31)

Here we see Jesus at his most agonisingly human. 'Now my heart is troubled . . . Father save me from this hour.' The greatest courage is surely that which knows its fate, feels the fear, and still goes ahead. Somehow it is a great comfort to know that Jesus struggled with fear, faced hard choices, and even wavered on the path. Bringing abundant life meant choosing death.

But he was quite clear about the momentousness of the choice. The world was in the balance – 'Now is the time for judgment on this world'.

Our world perhaps more than ever now is at a crossroads, faced with life and death choices. We have to choose between the destructive forces of war or peace; we have to choose between the starvation of growing numbers of our neighbours or a sharing of our resources; we have to choose between the degradation of the very planet we live on or the beauty of a harmonious existence. Many of the choices we make now are irreversible – life or death decisions for all time.

The nuclear clock on the *Bulletin of Atomic Scientists*, which gauges the state of nuclear peril, has just been moved two minutes closer to midnight. In a political climate where so many of the treaties carefully crafted for our safety are being torn up or ignored, it is indeed, as Martin Luther King said, 'Non-violence or non-existence'.

In March 2002 I was visiting church leaders in Angola as part of a joint Christian Aid/CAFOD delegation. Angola has been at war for over forty years and shows all the desperate ravages of savage fighting. The day we left the country a cease-fire was declared, and the Angolan churches were talking with hope and confidence about 'seizing the moment of opportunity' and working together to bring real lasting peace.

Helda is an Angolan woman pastor who works for Messengers for Peace. She told me about her work encouraging young men to refuse to fight. When I asked her if such activities were not treason and whether she was in danger of her life, she looked at me – grey-haired and wrinkly – and said, 'The Lord has given you thirty years of working for peace. I may only be allowed a few years, but I will die knowing that I have done the Lord's work.'

Lord, the world you have given us is a miracle of beauty, and yet we mar it and destroy it with our greed and ignorance. Restore in us a sense of reverence and wonder and give us a deep passion for justice, so that when we come to the difficult choices of life, our path may be clearer. And then we ask for your strength to uphold us.

Day 11

Seeing the Father
John 14:8–14

*If you really knew me, you would know
my Father as well. (John 14:7)*

Jesus must have been impatient sometimes that the disciples were such slow learners. 'Don't you know me, Philip, even after I have been among you such a long time?' Throughout his ministry with them Jesus had been demonstrating by his very life what God was like, and they could still ask, 'Show us the Father.'

It's understandable, really. After all, most of us do exactly the same. They saw a great teacher, storyteller, leader, companion, but they hadn't grasped that this totally human, vulnerable friend of theirs was God. Bringing God down to earth in this way is revolution and overturns all the awesomeness and inaccessibility of God, making God nearer than breathing.

The really hard bit to understand is that Jesus was saying that the very same power that was in him is in all of us as well. The kingdom of God is at hand – not in some distant unattainable future, but here and now in our own lives. Heaven and Hell as we create them on earth. We too, with all our frailties and flaws, are in the Father and the Father is in us. Jesus brings God right down to earth, and raises each one of us up to heaven.

The word 'Messiah' means 'anointed one', and there is a sense in which we are all anointed in the Spirit. At a point in my life when I was feeling particularly depressed about the state of the world, I attended a Western Orthodox service in Brussels on Palm Sunday. As we went forward to receive the elements in the

Eucharist, the priest anointed each of us in turn with an appropriate blessing. As he marked the sign of the cross on my forehead, he said, 'The oil of resistance'.

Because if we are indeed anointed as a people of God, who knows where the Spirit will lead us? If we drink this cup we become part of God's upside-down kingdom, and nothing is ever the same. It is an awe-inspiring challenge to know that God's power is available to us in full measure, but we will need every bit of it if we are to walk the road ahead.

> Lord, you have made us one with you through Jesus, and promised us the power and strength of the Spirit. Help us to feel the rushing mighty wind of this power, and give us the courage to follow where it leads. And we give thanks for the sheer adventure of your leading.

Day 12

ROBIN EAMES

Moving mountains
John 4:16–24

A time is coming when you will worship the
Father neither on this mountain nor in Jerusalem.
(John 4:21)

Working and worshipping in an environment such as Northern Ireland I am all too familiar with conflict which has a religious label. With roots far back in history, that conflict has of course many causes, and to talk only of a 'religious' war is over-simplification. There are strong political overtones and questions of identity for two communities. But the religious identity, Protestant or Roman Catholic, plays a profound role in our historic tragedy. We have come a long way to solving those tensions, but much remains to be addressed.

World history bears ample testimony to the consequences of religious conflict. Religious fanaticism through the ages has produced human suffering and death on a scale which asks deep questions about the true nature of religious belief. When political partisanship is added to the score the result has inevitably led to conflict.

Jesus goes to the root of religious bigotry as he talks to the Samaritan woman. The argument as to whether the mountain or Jerusalem was the correct location for worship raised much more than the nature of religious rivalry: it raised the whole question of religious prejudice and sectarianism. Above and beyond any argument based on self-centred interest the only true way to approach the Throne of Grace was 'to worship the Father in spirit and in truth'.

In the heat of a conflict situation some years ago a young man said to me, 'Why should we take on board the views of others – haven't we always done it this way?' His ancestors may have held their mountain to be sacred. The tragic truth was that there were others with their own special mountains who, like him, did not want to look to the faith or hopes of others.

Given the long history of religious/political conflict in this small part of the world, we may well wonder – will it ever change? This generation is struggling with what it means to be prisoners of history. But examples of great individual courage abound – people who are unafraid to say, 'It can't go on like this.' In their own way their faith is strong enough given encouragement to 'move mountains'.

The Christian faith of the resurrection continues to give hope that one day we will ask, 'Was it really as bad as that years ago?'

> God of all ages,
> who through your Son, Jesus Christ, draws all to the truth of
>   our oneness in your image:
> heal the wounds we have inflicted on each other in the name
>   of religion,
> and lead us to peace.
> Amen.

Day 13

The pride of self
Isaiah 58:1–9

'Why have we fasted,' they say, 'and you have not seen it?'
(Isaiah 58:3)

Religious rivalry is a particularly divisive characteristic of human nature. Beneath its recognisable consequences lie traditional seeds of self-righteousness.

Isaiah frequently draws on the evil of pious attitudes to pronounce on the blindness of seeing only 'our way', 'our path', 'our attitude', as the true way to spiritual peace and satisfaction. He writes of the dangers of doing as you please on the day of your fasting (v. 3).

Like the little child who proclaimed to her friends, 'My way is best – it's much better than yours,' adult life confronts us in many subtle ways with the sin of self-righteous pride. In our village today self-centred interest is not confined to everyday life in a local community. International relations are frequently dominated by determination to seek solutions only acceptable to one side or source. In a pluralist world those facts are of profound importance.

When we turn to worship, the danger of self-righteousness becomes real. Do you not see how sincerely we worship? Do you not recognise the tangible truths we hold? How long will it be until you realise how wrong you are when compared with our righteousness?

Even in our private prayers and devotions it is all too easy to seek a degree of personal pride in our own rightness. It is so often our solution to a problem, our will, our hope which God must recognise. We leave so little room for the will and purpose of God to become plain.

Surely we are called to see the goodness, truth and sincerity of others if our approach to God is to be removed from the pride of self?

Understanding someone else's religious experience is in my community frequently interpreted as weakness. In the sight of God, reconciliation is far from that. It is the real strength of recognising despite our differences that we are all made in his image.

Merciful Father,
lead us in your paths of truth
that we may see your love and glory
as much in the lives of others
as in our own journey to the cross.
Amen.

Day 14

Confronting idols
Isaiah 19:1–4, 19–24

The idols of Egypt tremble before [the Lord], and the hearts of the Egyptians melt within them. (Isaiah 19:1)

Isaiah was unafraid to confront idolatry, whether in Egypt or Damascus. In his Oracles he drew a distinction between true and false prophets. But his distinction went further. Allegiance to the truth of God could be tainted, even destroyed, by allegiance to false idols. Such idols would in time lead to destruction of self and destruction of a community.

Religious conflict frequently stems from belief and practice which has 'had its day'. We are all what history has made us. Each generation passes on its prejudices as well as its hopes to another. Here in my community people suffer injustice and misunderstanding because of the past. Truly we are all prisoners of our past – and we will continue to be until we recognise there are idols which must be confined to history.

Memory is one of the most significant influences in all our lives. Whether we realise it or not, memory is just as important an ingredient in what we are as any other factor. What really controls our outlook and attitude is what we do with our memories. How do we decide on those memories worth keeping and those we ought to throw into the waste-bin of the past?

Memories of hurt or insult, memories of perceived past injustice to us, or the like, all lead to bitterness as we confront the present or look to the future. Such emotions can easily become the idols to which we dedicate our lives. I have seen so many lives blighted, even ruined, by a failure to distinguish between what idol of our past is worthy of retention – and what must go for ever . . .

> *Lord of history,*
> *Lord of our past,*
> *Lord of our present,*
> *Lord of our future,*
> *speak to us in ways we will understand,*
> *speak to us in ways we can hear,*
> *point us towards the real truth which will endure.*
> *Amen.*

Day 15

Unhealthy rivalry
John 3:25–36

He is baptising, and everyone is going to him. (John 3:26)

John's disciples and the Jews found themselves in a bitter conflict over purifying, or religious washing. Rivalry was as much a consequence of contrasting loyalties and contrasting personalities as it was about religious doctrine. The suggestion was that somehow there was a competition for loyalty between the practices of John and Jesus. Where did the truth lie?

Throughout Christian history the belief that only some have a monopoly of respect and honour has driven wedges of mistrust and misunderstanding between people 'made in the image of the same God'. So it is today that the excessive importance or influence of one person in the family of the Church is too easily perceived to be a lowering of the value of another.

Where there is conflict based even partly on religious identity, one-upmanship plays its own insidious part. It is not always easy to accept that the role God gives to an individual which carries with it perceived importance lowers the role or influence of another. The gifts or opportunities granted to one do not in any way devalue the attributes of another fellow-pilgrim.

Give and take is a vital step in community as well as personal relationships. Where injustice for one community is addressed it must not lead to the belief that a sense of injustice in another is being ignored. Such perceptions in my experience are a real cause of community conflict. They also have something to say about how we view God's purposes rather than our own . . .

Grant to us
a clear vision of your purpose
for the gifts and opportunities we are given
and remove from us the envy and jealousy
which destroy respect for the needs and feelings of others
so that we may all rejoice in your love.
Amen.

Day 16

Rules or miracles?
John 5:1–18

My Father is always at his work to this very day.
(John 5:17)

The miracle of healing was lost on those who believed the Sabbath day was inappropriate for such an occurrence at the pool of Bethesda. The argument, once removed from the human need of the disabled man, revealed the hypocrisy of those who confused the power of godliness with their religious zeal for outward form. To them the method used was of greater importance than the spiritual content, the power of Christ of less significance than a perceived misuse of the Sabbath. Rules outweighed the inspiration of a miracle.

What a clear insight into human nature.

It is all too easy to blind ourselves to the hand of God in human affairs by relating such an occurrence to rules and regulations, community ethos or set patterns of behaviour rather than accepting the sheer majesty and wonder of his love.

Time and again in my work in Northern Ireland I have faced seemingly impossible difficulties of attitude or position when attempting to move a situation forward – only to be amazed by a turn of events which could only stem from the hand of God.

Situations where there was simply no hope of compromise, when suddenly one side or the other made a positive move. Situations where great sorrow or loss should have produced in human terms anger and bitterness but which in fact produced unbelievable examples of forgiveness or reconciliation. By the laws of this world little hope appeared possible. In the will and purposes of God, conflict turned into a miracle.

All of us suffer at times from the belief that we alone can produce solutions to human situations of loss or conflict. Who can possibly evaluate what the unfettered power of God can produce when we have the faith to place all in his hands – and learn to ignore the niceties of human rules?

Pour into our hearts
such a love towards you
that in every situation of life
we may allow your will, your purpose and your influence
to overcome our self-centred importance,
and grant us the humility to accept your will
rather than to cling to our own.
Amen.

Day 17

True worship
John 16:1–11

A time is coming when those who kill you will think they are offering a service to God. (John 16:2, NIV Inclusive)

True worship centres on waiting upon God. It is to the sheer majesty and power of God we must turn when we worship. Worship in that sense is the greatest privilege open to humankind.

The fourth Gospel contains clear indication of the dangers when we are unclear about the real purpose of worship. The practice of worship can be summed up in the traditional words, 'we must decrease that he increases'. The worshipper is reminded of unworthiness, sin and weakness as he or she kneels before God. The Old Testament spoke of looking at God rather than turning to God. St John's Gospel takes up that same theme, with the added dimension of the perfect love of an understanding God seen through the life and witness of Christ.

It is easy to think we are glorifying God when we presume to believe he is on our side. In this community at times both sides claim a monopoly of God's support. They talk of a Protestant God, a loyalist God – or a Roman Catholic or nationalist God. The laws of God are on their side and they have some divine right to embrace his strength for their particular cause. This is at the least a total misunderstanding of the nature of God, and at most blasphemy.

The universal nature of Almighty God cannot be interpreted in any sectional way. God is the God who reaches out in mercy, love and forgiveness to all his children and at all times. Only when we grasp this total universality of God do we approach worship in the right and only frame of mind.

'For God and Ulster,' proclaims a wall mural in Belfast. Religious conflict drags the sheer majesty of God and worship into the cauldron of sectarianism. It is when we come to see God as the Father of all that we make real steps to realising the eternal privilege and purpose of worship.

O God of love and majesty,
help us to approach you in true humility,
conscious of our unworthiness,
our sin
and our dependence on your everlasting love
for all of us,
wherever and whoever we are.
Amen.

Day 18

Oneness in God
John 17:20–6

*May they be brought to complete unity to let the world
know that you sent me. (John 17:23)*

C hrist's great prayer for the future of his Church lies at the
very centre of the ecumenical journey. The vision and indeed
the dream of one great body of believers united in form and
substance has remained the ultimate purpose of that journey which
today dominates so much inter-church activity and dialogue. What
it will mean in the end remains a source of constant controversy
for the world Church. While now we see through a glass darkly, it
is our belief all will be revealed in God's own time.

Where there is conflict, such words as reconciliation, accommo-
dation, understanding and the process of bridge-building between
communities, nations and individuals become vehicles for endeav-
our. Too often I have found that opposition to understanding
interprets peacemaking as weakness. For many, real strength lies
in maintaining a fixed and unmoveable position in which the views
of others are of no importance.

Behind Christ's prayer for his Church lies the earnest appeal to
those in any form of conflict. It is a further reference to his longing
to see an end to confrontation, war and tension. He prays that we
may be united in a resolve to reach understanding, to overcome
difference and to become truly one in him.

There is room for diversity and difference but each human
situation contains points of contact, points of agreement and a
basis for reconciliation. No conflict in human relations is beyond

36

resolution. There is an answer to every problem. The trouble is a lack of will to find it or a lack of courage to face up to what a solution will mean. This is as true in the broken human relationship or dispute between individuals as it is between communities. Healing is costly – but forgiveness in some form holds the key to the oneness that comes with understanding and the end of conflict.

As we seek solutions to religious conflict across this world, the real comfort we have is that we are doing the work of Christ. It is his will that we find the oneness, understanding of each other and reconciliation which speak yet again of the need of all – forgiveness in the sight of God.

> *Grant us, O God, a new vision of your will*
> *that one day we may all be one*
> *in love for you,*
> *respect for each other,*
> *understanding of what is important for each other,*
> *and in compassion for those who suffer*
> *through the ignorance or indifference of others.*
> *Amen.*

Day 19

WEEK 3: CONFLICT BETWEEN NATIONS
BERNARDINO MANDLATE

Loving the darkness
John 3:16–21

Light has come into the world, but people loved darkness instead of light because their deeds were evil.
(John 3:19, NIV Inclusive)

In recent times we have witnessed massacres, random killings, ethnic cleansing in proportions never seen before. In Mozambique we had a war of our own, created and funded by neighbouring states, which lasted many years, and it took the churches by surprise. Then they remembered that they hold the light of Jesus and that through that light they could lighten the darkness that covered our country. And so it was that, through their prayers and openness, politicians accepted to uphold the light and peace came to stay.

Some people seem to enjoy life in the dark and give all sorts of excuses to remain there. It is extremely difficult to help someone who chooses to be blind. Jesus experienced this stubbornness with the Pharisees, Sadducees and other lawmakers of his day, people who deliberately refused to see the light he was bringing to the world. They deliberately blindfolded themselves and fought against Jesus.

But some, like Nicodemus, sneaked out of their group to have a private conversation with Jesus about their own personal salvation. Not everyone refused to see the light.

Jesus had come to bring peace to the world and the world chose to ignore him. Even today, the world still chooses to ignore the light he brought and continues to fight against itself, nation against nation, faction against faction. The Gospel tells us the truth. People loved and still love darkness rather than light. There are those who know it all and will not accept help from anyone, no matter how wrong or how much in the dark they may be. We are becoming impotent to bring light into this dark world in which we now live. Yet the Church is called by the Gospel to bring people into light and truth so that the glory of God may be manifest in the life of communities and societies to which we belong. There is no better time than Lent to reflect on our lives and the lives of those around us. When we do so, nations will change the way they behave.

God, we love and we thank you for your love. We know some of our mistakes and we ask your forgiveness for them and for the mistakes we make unknowingly. Give us the wisdom and the courage to help change and transform the world into your ideal. Help us to be and to bring light and peace to our nations. Amen.

Day 20

This is what the king of Assyria says: Make peace with me
and come out to me. Then every one of you will eat from
your own vine and fig-tree and drink water from your own
cistern, until I come and take you to a land like your own –
a land of corn and new wine, a land of bread and vineyards.
(Isaiah 36:16–17)

Most of the countries in the Two-Thirds World have heard this kind of promise from many countries in the One-Third World. Promises of milk and honey, promises of better living conditions. Countries have been impoverished and indebted by this kind of promise, and unfortunately most of our leaders have fallen foul of these promises.

Since 1986, Mozambique has been implementing International Monetary Fund and World Bank programmes which promised better living conditions, more jobs and all that the poor need. The government told us to fasten our seatbelts and tighten our belts because we were in for a rough ride. And so it proved. Conditions got worse, and we drew our belts still tighter. No one eats from their own vine or fig-tree, no one drinks from their own cistern. Our land is no longer ours – the rich are grabbing it out of our hands. The promise of a better life never materialises.

Because of false promises, poverty has increased in our nations, preventable diseases have increased, and the ability to deal with them has decreased. Clean water cannot be provided for poor communities; people are not drinking from their own cisterns, they are compelled to drink from their pockets. Interestingly enough, not all our people in the Two-Thirds World have pockets. The promises are not materialising.

One needs to counter these and other false promises because they simply destroy life for many people. Why promise a land like your own instead of making life possible for people in their own land? We serve a God whose promises are real, they are there for us to grasp and enjoy. God has no hidden agendas in his dealings with us and he honours his promises. The king of Assyria was looking for an easy way out by making enticing promises. What he didn't know was that Hezekiah's God was not like the gods he thought he had defeated, and he could not stand in his way. We'll see tomorrow that Hezekiah prays and the Lord listens to him and answers his prayers. We can pray for ourselves and for the wellbeing of other peoples in all nations, and use God's wisdom to improve the lives of all.

Lord, make us aware of what surrounds us, so that we can distinguish between what is true and what is false. Help us to be truthful and to listen to your voice and not be cheated by false promises that do not yield any results.

Day 21

Now, O Lord our God, deliver us from his hand, so that
all kingdoms on earth may know that you alone,
O Lord, are God. (Isaiah 37:20)

This is a great prayer, perhaps offered out of fear of defeat by the enemy, but a great prayer nonetheless. And it could have been prayed out of a genuine trust in God, a God who never failed his people. Sometimes when I see all the wars between nations being waged in the name of God, I wonder who God is listening to, or on whose side he is fighting, if indeed he is involved in our wars at all.

When Hezekiah earnestly prayed to God, he was facing a huge Assyrian army which he knew he could not defeat and he put his trust in the Lord. He asked the Lord to fight his battle so that the world might know there is only one God. God answered this prayer in a mighty way, decimating the enemy army.

In Mozambique we prayed for the end of the war, and God in his way of listening to us showed us what to do to enable peace to come our way. We did that, and peace came. When we earnestly pray to God for what is right, God hears us and wants to respond. Sometimes the answer may not be exactly what we expected, but it is a response nonetheless. God may not smite armies fighting against us, but he may enable us to join peace processes that will bring to an end the wars we cannot win.

We are now involved in campaigns for debt cancellation, fair trade and other justice-related issues around the world, campaigns meant to improve the living conditions of poor people. These are wars which we need to pray earnestly to God to help us win. And God will enable us to win them, not just for our own sake but for his glory, so that the whole world may know he is the only true God, that there is no other through whom wars can be won. Ours is a loving and a listening God. No matter how bleak the situation may be, praying to God helps, and God is able to hear us. Let us trust him with our lives and destiny; let us open our eyes and our hearts and we'll see what the Lord can do for us.

Lord, in the same way that you heard and responded to Hezekiah's prayer, so we ask you to hear and answer us. We have so many wars that we need to win for our people's sake and for your glory's sake. You know our weaknesses, you know where we falter. Come to our aid, Lord, help us shape the world better. Lord, in your mercy, hear our prayer.

Day 22

God's warrior
Isaiah 45:1–8

You heavens above, rain down righteousness; let the clouds shower it down. Let the earth open wide, let salvation spring up, let righteousness grow with it; I, the Lord, have created it.
(Isaiah 45:8)

God has always used human beings as instruments for his work. Cyrus was chosen and anointed by God to free God's people, to conquer and subdue nations on God's behalf. When God does that, it is not for the sake of the chosen individual, but for God himself and for his people. So humans become instruments in the hands of God.

It is through his chosen instruments that God blesses the whole world and everyone in it. When God's righteousness rains down it does so on everyone. It is like rain when the heavens open. It falls alike on the fields of those who follow him and on the fields of those who deny him, and the effect is the same: more crops are yielded to feed the world.

Our God is a God of salvation, salvation for all humankind. He wants us to own this salvation for ourselves, to allow it to spring up in us and others, and to accompany salvation with peace and justice for all. We may be his chosen and anointed ones for our time. We have to try to do the kind of things God would have us do. When we embark on campaigns for a better world for all its inhabitants, we are doing God's work that needs to be done, and if we drop out we fail God and we fail those who inhabit the world with us – we do the whole world a disservice. We could be the Cyruses of our time, but we won't know until the work is done.

God can give us the strength we need, to perform all the things we need to do, for the wellbeing of society. Some people still believe that the Church has a part to play in the world order. Questions like 'What is the Church doing about this or that?' are still being asked when things are not right in society. Do we have anything to say about HIV/AIDS? The Church may have an important role in reducing the spread of the pandemic, a role which is not being properly fulfilled at the moment, with conflicting messages coming out of the churches. In this case we may be the modern Cyrus, modern warriors who will save God's people from this disease. May we be able to trust in God.

> *Lord, we are your servants. Show us what you want us to do to help save your people from the difficult situations in which they find themselves. We want to be honest and faithful to you, Lord: help us in our endeavour. Give us the strength we need to continue fighting for the wellbeing of your people and ourselves.*

Day 23

You have trusted in your wickedness and have said,
'No one sees me.' Your wisdom and knowledge mislead
you when you say to yourself, 'I am, and there is
none besides me.' (Isaiah 47:10)

A well-known African proverb says that 'I am because you are and you are because I am'. There is an interrelatedness in human beings that makes them dependent on each other. No one can live in isolation from others. No matter how clever or powerful one may be, as humans we will always need one another. We are a community people.

There are many powerful nations, well-equipped militarily and rich economically, who sometimes threaten smaller nations. Very often even they need the assistance of other nations to be able to do their dirty work.

Our pride sometimes makes us think we can do whatever we want without the help of others, but there will always be something we cannot do on our own. We need each other to make it through life. It is from others that we learn what we know. It is through the experience of others that we may avoid making mistakes. If we neglect other people's knowledge we are bound to fail and fall, and when that happens we will need other people's hands to enable us to stand on our feet again.

A group of young people came to Mozambique to help the churches with some small projects, which included erecting a two-roomed building. Local people were at hand to help. A suggestion was made by one of the locals as to how to go about putting up the building. This was local knowledge at its best. But the young visitors ignored it because they thought they knew better. The building was put up and the roof was put on. A few weeks later the building collapsed from the top down, and local people had to do it their way. We need each other and we need to respect each other. *Together we stand, divided we fall.*

God sees us, no matter where we hide. We are created in his image and thus we see God every day, although we may not recognise him in the faces of so many people we meet and neglect in our lives. How I wish we could all set our pride aside and face life with the rest of humanity to build a common life for all.

Lord, humble us, mould us to be like you, to live your life according to God's will. On our own we are useless, weak and unable to do anything of worth for you or for our fellow human beings. We rely on your love, care and guidance. Use us, Lord, as you will.

Day 24

Returning from exile
Isaiah 52:1–10

How beautiful on the mountains are the feet of those who bring good news, who proclaim peace, who bring good tidings, who proclaim salvation, who say to Zion, 'Your God reigns!' (Isaiah 52:7)

There is a village back home called Hokwe, which I used to visit on my pastoral duties. And it so happened that whenever I went there a few drops of rain would fall, and sometimes it rained hard. People in that village always wanted me to visit. They may have learned to like me as well, but I often thought that they wanted me to visit because they would get some rain while I was there. In a way I was the bearer of good news for that small community.

The Christian Church has been entrusted with the good news of Jesus Christ to spread far and wide. In many communities around the world, the Church and its workers have been regarded as the bearers of good news. One wonders, though, whether today those communities would still see the feet of the Church and its workers as beautiful. When the Church becomes part of the problem, rather than the vehicle for its lasting solution, her feet cannot be so beautiful. Just recall the cases of Burundi and Rwanda where people were killed on church premises.

How would we want our church to be seen in our communities today: as part of the solution or part of the problem? In Mozambique politicians respect the Church, and when the Church intervenes they listen, because when it mattered the Church could put its pride aside and brought peace to the country. That makes the feet of the Church beautiful because there is often good news coming from it. Many people in exile returned home through the good offices of the Church, and the Church spread her arms wide to welcome them back. They thanked God for the Church's intervention in bringing peace and in helping them come back home to start their lives anew. We too live in exile, the exile of our lives, and wonder when God will help us to come back where we belong. We belong with him, and yet we trust that our material possessions will be enough and we have no need for God. Why did so many people attend church services after the events of 11 September? Because suddenly they realised that there was a spiritual emptiness in their lives that needed to be filled. Are we feeling like that still?

> *Lord, help us to swallow our pride and be your instruments for peace and justice. There are many good things we know we can do, but often our pride stops us from acting. Show us your ways, so that people may see you at work in us and follow you.*

Day 25

Trusting in God
Isaiah 12:1–6

Sing to the Lord, for he has done glorious things;
let this be known to all the world. (Isaiah 12:5)

Indeed the Lord does do great things if we allow him space to operate. Human beings need to learn to listen to God and to allow him the space and the opportunity to be active in our lives. When we do that, we'll have every reason to sing praises to God, because we shall be doing it out of our own experience. It was through earnest prayer that God gave a vision to the Mozambican churches, a vision of peace and unity for the country. God gave the vision and showed the way to make that vision a reality. There were a lot of sacrifices to be made, but it was worth it because eventually peace was achieved.

Since then the churches have made a point of celebrating the day of peace, which has now become a national holiday. This is a celebration of something to which the Church made a huge contribution because it listened to the Lord. It is a celebration of praise to God because he did great things for our nation.

Now the Mozambican churches share their experiences with other churches in other countries where conflict abounds. When one nation achieves peace for its citizens, that peace is shared by other nations, in particular the neighbouring ones, and we all praise the Lord for enabling these achievements.

The Lord wants to do great things for us and he does so through human beings, who become his instruments. If world leaders would listen to and trust what God has to say about the world order, and if they had the political will to follow his ordinances, many of the conflicts that surround us would be overcome not by military might, but by the love and grace which ought to be the main characteristics of humanity. It is pointless saying 'in God we trust' if we do not care to listen to him and follow him.

We who follow him ought to be able to sing praises to God for the wonderful things he does for humanity in spite of humans having lost their humane-ness. We also need to put our trust in the Lord, and trust him with the course of history. We could do better if that trust were there. Do we care to trust in our God?

Lord, you continue to show your greatness to us through your love and care. For our own good you choose not to see the rottenness in us. You continue to be a forgiving God. Give us the courage and the heart to proclaim your glory and to exalt your name throughout the world, so that every soul may know that you are the Lord.

WEEK 4: WAR AND PEACE AT THE END OF THE AGE

ANDREW GODDARD

An otherworldly kingdom
John 18:28–40

My kingdom is not of this world. If it were, my servants would fight to prevent my arrest. (John 18:36)

'My kingdom is not of this world.' This famous saying of Jesus is one that Christians often seriously misunderstand. Regularly it is used to suggest that the Church, if it is to be faithful to Jesus, should be focused on a world other than this one. The kingdom which Christians proclaim and which directs our vision is then called 'heavenly' and understood to be something wholly beyond and disconnected from this mortal and material life.

When we read these words in that way we forget that they are explained by John's Gospel as a whole and particularly by the words that immediately follow. Jesus goes on to explain that if his kingdom was of this world then his servants would fight to defend him. Reading on, we find a quite different explanation for this 'otherworldliness' which faces us with two challenges.

The first challenge lies in Jesus' reminder to us that the goal of human history, the restoration of God's good creation, the kingdom of Christ, is not something established by force of arms. Why is his kingdom 'not of this world'? Not because it leaves no mark on this world. It is 'not of this world' because – in contrast to all the kingdoms of this world – Christ rejects violence as the way of leaving his mark on the world. His kingdom comes to us instead as a gift, 'from another place', and we who follow him are called to witness to this truth (v. 37).

Then, second, in our world racked with war and violence this verse also challenges our basic presupposition that the most important things in life are things we should fight for. Again and again, presidents, prime ministers, freedom fighters and the media seek to enlist us in the service of war by expressing our political conflicts in terms of the ultimate – a fight for peace, for freedom, for justice, for good against evil. But here (v. 37) King Jesus calls on those of us who acknowledge his lordship to reject all such talk as lies, and to testify instead to the Truth who has come into the world and saved it without recourse to sword or bomb or landmine.

King Jesus, when the rulers of this world seek to establish their kingdoms by force, strengthen us to remain faithful witnesses to your kingdom of peace and justice until the day when the kingdoms of the world become the kingdom of our Lord and you reign for ever and ever.

Day 27

Devastation
Isaiah 24:1–13

The earth will be completely laid waste and totally plundered. (Isaiah 24:3)

Much of the Bible is not pleasant, not easy. But then much of life in our world is neither pleasant nor easy so that shouldn't surprise us. Brutal wars. Terrorist threats. Ethnic cleansing. Environmental disaster. Famine. Most of us can live our daily lives not directly threatened by such dangers. But many people around God's world have no need of an act of imagination or a television screen for the frightening words of these verses to come to life. Isaiah's description is horribly close to daily reality.

That is grim enough, but we don't need a prophet to tell us what the world is like. What the prophet needs to tell us is something even more unsettling. We are ultimately all in this together. Whatever our social or economic status, we cannot escape our responsibility or think we can avoid the consequences of our actions. We are all caught up in this together because we all contribute in various ways to the mess the world is in. We have all defiled the earth and broken the covenant between God and all his creatures (v. 5). In an age when we speak more and more of globalisation and the reality of living in one world, Isaiah reminds us of the global reign and power of sin and its stranglehold on human societies.

If that were not disturbing enough, the prophet boldly speaks of God at work in and through such horrors. When the whole world and its economic and political systems reject the God of

Israel and become enthralled to evil, the Lord will not sit back and do nothing. He will mount an assault on evil and act in judgment, even when that means the earth will be completely laid waste (v. 3). He will break into our joyful revelries (vv. 7–8). He will break down all we proudly build and look to for protection and security (vv. 10, 12). And when it is the Lord who acts in judgment the rich and powerful and secure will find they can no longer construct escape routes (vv. 1–3). For the wrath of God is being revealed from heaven (Romans 1:18).

> *Kyrie eleison.*
> *God our Father, we confess that our choices and lifestyles sustain the economic and political injustice of our world. Open our eyes that we might see ourselves and our world as you see us. Change our hearts and strengthen our hands that we might struggle against our sin. And in your anger, Lord, remember mercy. Through Jesus Christ our Lord.*

Day 28

The bigger picture
Isaiah 24:14–23

The moon will be abashed, the sun ashamed; for the Lord Almighty will reign on Mount Zion and in Jerusalem, and before its elders, gloriously. (Isaiah 24:23)

After yesterday's bleak opening we might think at first that things are looking up. There are shouts of joy. Singing returns to the earth after it had been silenced (vv. 14–16a). But this is only a brief and puzzling respite before the prophet's terrifying words begin again. Soon we are reminded that there will be no escape for anyone from this universal catastrophe (vv. 17–18) with vivid imagery in which the whole earth gets shaken to its core and is left staggering around like a disoriented drunk (vv. 19–20a).

That cycle is sadly familiar to us. We think we have found peace and resolved some area of conflict in our world, only for everything to fall to pieces once again as we stagger into some new cycle of violence and bloodletting. And once again we are reminded of two underlying causes – human sin and rebellion (v. 20b) and the active judgment of the Lord (v. 21).

But like other pieces of apocalyptic literature in Scripture, notably Revelation, these verses also give us a bigger picture, a vision of hope in a world that is falling apart and breaking up. They invite us to view events in terms of competing powers and assure us that God ultimately reigns. Our lives now are shaped and governed by spiritual and political forces, 'the powers in the heavens above and the kings on the earth below' (v. 21) that reap destruction across the whole of God's earth. The day will come, however, when those powers will be overthrown, imprisoned and punished by the earth's true Lord (vv. 21–2). In that day even the brightness of the sun and moon will fade, for the Lord will reign and, amazingly, he will reign on the earth. The earth which appeared to have been shattered into pieces has not been totally destroyed. That could never be the plan and purpose of the creator God. As in the days of Noah, a remnant has survived. God has not forgotten his covenant people. Jerusalem, Mount Zion and the elders have been preserved (v. 23). On that day, when Christ returns, God's glory will at last be manifest on the earth.

Maranatha. Come, Lord Jesus.
Faithful God, help us to understand that our struggle is not against flesh and blood but against the principalities and powers in the heavenly realms. Keep us faithful in prayer so that when the Son of Man comes he will find faith on the earth.

Day 29

*The Sovereign Lord will wipe away the tears
from all faces. (Isaiah 25:8)*

Among the many shocking scenes on 11 September 2001 was one of street celebrations in parts of the Occupied Territories. Many of us in the West couldn't understand how anyone could ever respond to such horror and devastation with joy and delight. And yet these verses call for a similar sort of response by God's people to the horrors and devastation described in the previous chapter – 'I will exalt you and praise your name . . . you have done marvellous things . . . you have made the city a heap of rubble' (vv. 1, 2). What can be going on here?

Those on the margins, those who have been abused, cannot but celebrate God's liberating judgment which demonstrates the Lord is a refuge to the poor and needy (v. 4). But that very judgment – as at the Red Sea – also destroys systems of power and silences the songs of the ruthless (v. 5). Walter Brueggemann sums up these unsettling verses with the chilling words, 'This poem is the voice of the poor and needy, who regard the demise of exploitative urban civilization as a gain and a gift from Yahweh.'[2]

But the real cause of joy cannot be found in the horrific destruction. This is not approval for history's sorry story in which the oppressed celebrate their victory by becoming the new oppressors. The celebration is not even simply at the vindication of the oppressed. The joy is produced by the destiny which, in contrast to 11 September, surely follows when it is *God's* action of judgment. Mount Zion now becomes the place of a new society. Instead of division and inequality, oppression and violence, there will be feasting and thanksgiving, a true eucharistic community (v. 6). And, in contrast to the earlier revelries of the rich and powerful, this is an inclusive and universal community where there is rich food and the best wine given to 'all peoples'. Here, at last, 'all faces' will have their tears wiped away as the power of death which covered 'all peoples' and ruled through them is swallowed up by God for ever (vv. 7–8). This is our God. We trusted him. He saved us. Let us rejoice and be glad in his salvation.

Gracious Father, open our ears to the cries of the poor, the oppressed and victims of violence and war. May all who long for the current world system to be brought crashing to the ground find their hope in you and discover amongst your people the gift of life shared freely and with great joy. Amen.

Day 30

Trust and obey
Isaiah 26:1–10

You will keep in perfect peace those whose minds are steadfast, because they trust in you. (Isaiah 26:3)

Looking out on our world full of violence and conflict, is there no peace until the day of God's final judgment? These verses show that, even in the midst of chaos and reversal, we not only have a future hope but a present peace. Such peace is, however, not a peace the earthly city can give. Those who invest themselves in that city and its boasts to bring peace will find that, in words echoed in Mary's Magnificat, the Lord 'humbles those who dwell on high, he lays the lofty city low' (v. 5). That city will be brought so low that those viewed as the lowest of its low will no longer find the city overshadowing them; they will trample it underfoot (v. 6).

True peace in this world comes only from another city, a strong city whose boundaries are marked out and secured by God's salvation (v. 1). True peace is God's shalom. Not simply the absence of war but the right ordering and flourishing of all that God has made. That true peace is God's gift to those who, even when surrounded by military, economic, political and ecological catastrophes, put their trust in the Lord, the Rock eternal (vv. 3, 4). That peace the world can neither give nor take away.

The trust which secures us such peace is not, however, some naïve escapist optimism which turns a blind eye to the world collapsing around about us. It is not simply the power of positive thinking. Whoever trusts also obeys, walking in the ways of the Lord (v. 8), the ways of righteousness and the paths of justice

(Proverbs 8:20) that contrast with the unjust ways of the world. And whoever trusts and obeys also waits eagerly for the Lord's coming. For only the advent of the Lord, not some military operation or even UN peacekeepers, can bring an end to our plight and teach the peoples of the earth righteousness (v. 9). And such trust, obedience and patient hope is only breathed into life and can only be kept alive by our heart's desire for God – his name, his renown, his very self (vv. 8, 9).

> God our Father, as we work for peace in your warring world may we faithfully follow the path of the Prince of Peace and be filled with his Spirit of peace, until he comes again and the whole earth is filled with the knowledge of the Lord as the waters cover the sea. Amen.

Day 31

Mere mortals
Isaiah 26:11–27:1

We have not brought salvation to the earth.
(Isaiah 26:18)

As the Bible repeatedly reminds us, from the story of Babel onwards, we humans constantly get too high an opinion of ourselves. In our day and age, our technological prowess and our global networks of communication make us even more confident in our ability to improve the world. In contrast, Lent is a time of putting things aside, being stripped down, learning to be in the desert. These verses show us just how powerless we really are and, in contrast, how powerful is our God.

We constantly seek to deny, hide and overcome it, but the simple fact is that all our human powers are limited by our mortality. Of all those who appear to be movers and shakers on the world stage, of history-makers, of everyone listed among the world's wealthiest and richest, of me and of you, it will one day be said, 'They are now dead, they live no more' (v. 14).

But even while we are alive, we constantly find our plans foiled, our hopes dashed and our visions brought to nought. Isaiah takes the powerful image of a woman in the pains of childbirth, writhing and crying out in agony (v. 17). This is a process of great suffering but it is a bearable suffering because it is a process with great promise, the promise of new life. But not now and not here. Here and now we by ourselves only give birth to . . . wind (v. 18). Again and again we think that through the struggles of developing and enacting our political programmes, our military manoeuvres and our medical technologies, we will be able to rescue ourselves and put our world to rights. Again and again we have to confess, 'We have not brought salvation to the earth' (v. 18).

Is there, then, no hope? Of course there is hope. The Lord himself will destroy the great sea monster who symbolises all that brings chaos and disorder to his world (27:1). But what of us? Can't our human deeds achieve anything? Of course we can make a difference. But we are to act not with pride in our own strength but with the humble confession, 'all that we have accomplished you have done for us' (26:12).

> Lord God, we confess that even if we do all that we are commanded we remain unworthy servants. In all our works for justice and peace, protect us from pride and teach us humility, that in the last day when your kingdom comes on earth we may hear your gracious words, 'Well done, good and faithful servant'. In the name of our servant king, Jesus Christ.

Day 32

Called to peace
Isaiah 27:2–13

Let them make peace with me. (Isaiah 27:5)

These chapters from Isaiah have not been comfortable reading. They highlight that, because God is not indifferent but passionate, he cannot turn a blind eye to our rejection of him and our inhumanity towards each other. He judges our human pride and oppression. This final reading also contains terrifying images of destruction (vv. 7–10) and warns that those who reject God cannot expect his compassionate favour (v. 11). It opens and closes, however, with words revealing God's heart and his purpose for our world.

The opening verses contrast sharply with the more famous vineyard of Isaiah 5:1–7. There we were reminded that God's chosen people are not exempt from his judgment when they are faithless. Here we see a different picture. Here we find God tending and caring for his precious vineyard (v. 3). Here we see that God sets himself to protect his vineyard by destroying all that would come against it to harm it (v. 4). Here we have the proclamation of the good news, 'I am not angry' (v. 4). God's wrath, though real, is his peculiar work faced with our sin and injustice. It is never a fixed and settled hostility towards us. Far from it, his great purpose and great plea is that in the midst of the terrors and conflicts by which we humans make history we should find our refuge in him (v. 5). His call, repeated to emphasise its importance, is that we now make peace with him (v. 5). It is a call made most fully to us in Jesus Christ. A call the Church is itself called to make as God's ambassador to a warring world, 'We implore you on Christ's behalf: Be reconciled to God' (2 Corinthians 5:20).

Those who heed that call to peace are not promised an easy life. They are certainly not guaranteed escape from the harsh realities of the world. In fact, they will often find themselves 'perishing' and 'exiled'. But whatever happens, their destiny is secure. God's purpose for all those who make their peace and are reconciled to him is clear. Whatever befalls them, they will reach the goal for which we were all made – they 'will come and worship the Lord' (v. 13).

Creator of all, our nation and our world are scarred by divisions and hatred. Make us your agents of reconciliation. Transform your Church to be the place where there is neither Jew nor Greek, slave nor free, male nor female, so that the world may know you call every nation, tribe, people and language to worship you through Jesus Christ our Lord.

Day 33

RAMANI LEATHARD

The greatest love
John 15:12–17

Love each other as I have loved you. Greater love has no-one than this, that he lay down his life for his friends.
(John 15:13)

Jesus instructs his disciples, his friends, to display Christ-like love, and in his impending death he will lay down his life for them. However, every human being is called into friendship with Christ and so his life is offered in sacrifice for the sins of the whole world. God's love is embodied in the sacrifice of Jesus, and in turn Christ's love for his friends will become known through his death.

The concept of sacrificial love is woven throughout the passion narrative. For me the concept was brought home intensely in Bangladesh a few years ago. In the Kulna district in the southwest, on 7 November every year, thousands of Bangladesh's poorest people in the area commemorate the death of a woman named Karuna. Karuna's memory has become synonymous with the cost of commercial prawn farming.

Twelve years ago, Karuna was among several hundreds from her village and fourteen surrounding villages taking part in a peaceful demonstration against the expansion of intensive prawn farming for export. Karuna and her neighbours did not want the salt water necessary for such intensive aquaculture to destroy their fertile rice fields and good pasture. Strangers from outside the community, paid thugs according to local observers, began attacking the crowd. Home-made bombs were used, and one of these bombs killed Karuna and injured many of her friends.

Sorrow at the death of their fellow-villager today gives strength to these farmers in attempting to change their future. Through Karuna's death, hope and liberation can be achieved in the same way that we are all set free through the death and resurrection of Christ. Karuna's neighbours continue to campaign in their small way, persuading the government and big farmers not to embark on intensive prawn farming. They try to show them that reverting to small-scale production based on traditional methods and without the intensive use of chemicals can prevent pollution of the land and water.

We hear nothing of the suffering or sacrifices of such ordinary people, like us trying to feed, house, clothe, educate and give health to their families, desperate to live in dignity with hope and purpose. They too hunger and thirst for righteousness, watching their world die around them or taking the risk of endangering their own lives, that others through the giving of their energy, skill and bodies might live – the way of Christ. Greater love has no one than this.

> Lord Jesus, you call us into friendship,
> Risky, daring friendship;
> Give us grace and courage to respond,
> Open our eyes to see you in the world,
> Open our arms to embrace you in our sisters and brothers,
> Open our minds to engage with today's painful issues,
> Open our hearts to love you in laying down self for you, our
>   friend.

Day 34

Life before death
John 12:1–8

Why wasn't this perfume sold and the money given to the poor? (John 12:5)

Monetary value cannot be attached to acts of generosity. Responding to the generous nature of God spurs us on to fight poverty. Here Mary is seen anointing Christ's feet with expensive perfume, but this generous act prompts Judas to question why the money was not spent on relief for the poor. Mary has done nothing wrong; indeed, her act of generosity is respected by Jesus when he says, 'Leave her alone.'

At the time of Jesus it was customary to anoint the body of a dead person, yet Mary carries out the act of anointing Jesus when he is still very much alive – perhaps a recognition that she already understood him to be the resurrection and the life. And in the death and raising of Lazarus we have had a foretelling of Christ's own death.

Christian Aid's commitment to 'life before death' reflects a vision of enabling every human being to live life in all its fullness. This is exactly what Mary was attempting to do in this episode. She, in her own way, was giving of herself most generously, and God accepts our gifts, prayers and actions, whatever they may be. What matters is how we use the potential we have to give of ourselves.

Babu and Adhilakshmi are human beings no different from us. They too have hopes and dreams, as we do. They are 'dalits' – outcastes in India's caste-ridden society. But as manual scavengers, an occupation carried out only by dalits, they are compelled to carry out the most demeaning activities. It is their responsibility to clean up and dispose of human excrement, to scour out dry latrines and large septic tanks. Neither of them has had a formal education, but they are determined to seek the best for their children and ensure that they are given the opportunity to study – so that they may have life before death.

Adhilakshmi is determined to work all the hours she can. It is a sacrifice she is willing to make so that her children can live in dignity. She says, 'It is undignified work, but there is no other way. Our children should not work like us. With the sacrifice we are making they can study. Our dreams are that our children should have a dignified and decent life.'

> Generous God, you give us everything,
> Our world, our humanity, our peace.
> May we mirror your generosity in our living
> Through our solidarity, prayers and action.
> May all your children find dignity and life in all its fullness.

Day 35

Betrayal
John 18:1–11

*I told you that I am he ... If you are looking for me,
then let these men go ... Shall I not drink the cup
the Father has given me? (John 18:8, 11)*

As we reflect on Jesus of Nazareth during Passiontide, we can explore for ourselves the way God might be calling us to live. 'You shall have no other gods before me,' asserts the first commandment. Put God first – the rejection of self, losing your life so you can gain it. The stark message of the cross is that our true power is found only when we take on the powerlessness of Christ crucified.

In these verses we read of the betrayal of Jesus. In Greek, the word 'betrayal' can simply mean 'to hand over'. It does not necessarily carry the same weight of guilt as in English. The passage is also about accepting responsibility and not leaving fate to others. Jesus did not wait to be identified, he came forward to face his own fate and take responsibility for what he was charged to do: 'Shall I not drink the cup the Father has given me?' (v. 11).

So it is with our own lives. Take the example of Reuben, a Methodist minister serving in Jeevodayam Farm, northwest Sri Lanka, which is home to sixty-five internally displaced Sri Lankan families. These families are refugees as a result of over two decades of ethnic conflict. The farm provides a haven of peace in the middle of war for the many who have been traumatised by the seemingly endless conflict. Reuben and the workers on the farm have been threatened many times. However, over the past few years, as a result of the work of the farm Reuben and the church have come to be trusted by both the army and the Tamil Tigers. Reuben is recognised as a man of peace and is convinced that his calling is to work among the vulnerable and needy. His words bear this out when he says, 'I feel that I need to work for the kingdom of God amid these people, a kingdom based upon peace, justice and harmony. So many of God's children in this area have been wounded and have suffered greatly, they need to be shown Christ's love.'

The Bishop of Colombo, the Rt Revd Duleep de Chickera, echoed these sentiments when alluding to the agreement on a cease-fire between the government of Sri Lanka and the Liberation Tigers of Tamil Eelam. He said that 'the distinct Christian contribution to the peace process is through truth and forgiveness without which there can be no reconciliation'.

Help us to remember today, Lord, that there is nothing we
*   cannot face together.*
How often will we betray you today Lord?
Ignoring our children's questions, walking past the Big Issue
*   seller.*
Turning off the news.
Shaking our heads at wars far away.
Little betrayals, handing you over.
Turn us again, Lord, to drink the cup of salvation
That we may die to self and live for you.

Day 36

I said nothing in secret. Why question me?
Ask those who heard me. Surely they know what I said.
(John 18:20–1)

Jesus' own words indicate that he has spoken out in public and those who heard him could vouch for what he has said and done. But this is not the case with everyone – take Peter.

In the courtyard, conflict rages around Peter. He is caught between a rock and a hard place. He has a desire to acknowledge Jesus and yet at the same time he is afraid that such acknowledgement will mark him out. It is as if this tension drives Peter further into darkness. Certainly his denial does not release him from it. Ironically, the crowing of the cock, which is a sign of the day dawning and therefore of light, is the time of deepest darkness for this disciple. However, this crippling fear is in contrast to the questioning in the resurrection narrative (John 21:15–19), when Peter is portrayed affirming his love for Jesus.

In the Philippines, Ned de Guzman is the director of an organisation called the Mindoro Association for Human Advancement and Linkages, or MAHAL (literally meaning 'love' in Tagalog). Ned and his wife Tita work tirelessly through MAHAL on the island of Mindoro to make communities aware of their rights, bringing people together to speak out for justice, to build self-reliant communities and to work for a fairer world. They are helping the villagers in Mindoro to preserve their livelihood of fishing and farming which is under threat from multinational mining companies. Individual farmers and fishermen in the villages of Mindoro have the odds stacked high against them, but with support they not only cope with their circumstances but have proved that they can speak out and even change the attitudes of governments and leaders around them.

Ned believes in a society where justice prevails. 'People need to be as well informed as possible in order to make choices that affect their lives. There are still so many injustices within our society. What is more frightening than the reign of evil is that no one speaks out against evil.' This is where our responsibility begins. We need not be afraid to speak out, for the good news is not secret but is there to be shared.

> God our Creator, we give you thanks for lips that we might speak.
> God our Saviour, give us the courage to overcome our fear so we might use our lips in service to speak out against evil.
> God our Sustainer, help us to walk in your way and work towards your reign where justice and peace prevail.

Day 37

Forgiveness
John 21:15–19

Lord, you know all things; you know that I love you.
(John 21:17)

In Matthew, Mark and Luke, discipleship begins when Jesus challenges his hearers, 'Follow me.' However in John's Gospel it is in light of the resurrection that Peter is told to follow Jesus. It is as if John is saying that true discipleship flows from the death and resurrection of the Lord. Jesus puts three questions to Peter, echoing Peter's threefold denial of him on the night of the trial. The threefold affirmation of love in this passage mirrors the complete turn-around that has occurred in Peter. We are shown how forgiveness makes for reconciliation.

Tu Lar Paw is a refugee. Her story is typical of many Karenni refugees from Burma who make the perilous journey across the border into Thailand in order to escape torture, rape and forced labour by the State Peace and Development Council (SPDC). Her home in Burma was burned down twice by the authorities and she had to flee into the jungle. She has been in Thailand since 1989 and is the chair of the Karenni refugee committee based in one of the camps along the border.

Being a Christian in a country where Christianity is a minority faith, Tu Lar Paw is aware of the importance of being tolerant of all faiths. She says: 'In my work it is vital that I respect people regardless of their faith. As Christians, through the Lord's Prayer, we are charged to be forgiving or we will never move forward, but it is very difficult to do, especially when I remember how we suffered at the hands of the military. Right now my prayer is that all my fellow refugees will continue to have their daily bread – or rice in our case – and for the deliverance of my people and for the leaders – for all those who are unable to cross the border in time. But I also pray for the SPDC, that they may walk the path of compassion and peace – as Jesus said, 'Thy will be done on earth as in heaven . . . forgive us our sins as we forgive others.'

In the pain of the tortured and in the loneliness of the refugee,
In the arrogance of the strong and in the security of the powerful,
In the comfort of my life and in the material bounty which cannot satisfy,
You ask me Lord, 'Do you love me?'
'Do you love me?'
'Do you love me?'
Forgive me, heal me, that I might dare to say, 'Yes.'

Day 38

*They divided my garments among them and cast lots
for my clothing. (John 19:24)*

According to Roman law, a person's clothes, taken off prior to
crucifixion, were handed over to the soldiers or guard as
booty. Here we are told that the soldiers cast lots to lay claim to
the various garments. It is then revealed that when Jesus was
stripped of his clothes, the soldiers discovered that the under-
garment or tunic he wore was a seamless robe, such as worn by a
high priest. It is symbolic that it is only when Jesus is stripped and
has nothing left but his humanity that his true status as high
priest is revealed. The layers are peeled off to reveal the truth. We
learn best when nothing is hidden. Indeed, the poor are our best
teachers.

While the guards on duty were divided about what to do with
Jesus' clothes, John attempts to point out that the death of Jesus
will not destroy the unity of the people who have gathered around
him. Perhaps we have here a hint that Israel's fulfilment is to
be found in the acknowledgment of Jesus as Messiah and the
fellowship of the Church. A recognition of the fact that Judaism
and Christianity are incomplete without each other and that they
are in fact mutually dependent.

The soldiers dividing Christ's clothing stand in contrast to the
frightened disciples, John and Mary the mother of Jesus, at the
foot of the cross. For while division is the order of the day for the
soldiers, each looking to his personal gain, Jesus, even in the agony

of crucifixion, restores divided humanity as he commends John and Mary into each other's care. Love for my neighbour makes me truly human.

We depend on each other, and how important it is that despite our diversity we are one mutually dependent world. Consider the amazing Jubilee 2000 movement, that was aimed at cancelling the billions of dollars of debt owed by the world's poorest countries. A great deal has been achieved, and yet it began from a small idea and mushroomed into a huge movement, thanks to people acting together.

One of the most crucial issues faced by Bangladesh today is that of natural arsenic contamination in the water supply – said to be the largest ever mass poisoning of a population. Christian Aid's Bangladesh partners have joined hands to form a network which aims to ensure access to safe water for all. This is a huge development challenge, but we know how with unified prayers and actions new life is possible. Bangladesh's challenge is for us all. We need to dig deep into our resources of justice, prayer and generosity to become a fountain of living water, welling up for the good of all creation.

Give us courage to tread the path of compassion and justice, to recognise that we are all one in your eyes. Help us to take up the challenges put before us in the knowledge that we can make a difference by coming together to work towards a common goal so that all may rejoice in your glorious resurrection.

Day 39

City of peace
John 14:25–31

Peace I leave with you; my peace I give you. I do not give to you as the world gives. (John 14:27)

Jesus uses the traditional word of greeting, *shalom* in Hebrew or *salaam* in Arabic, which translates as 'peace'. This is still very much the manner in which most people in the Holy Land greet each other today.

As we read of Christ's last few days in Jerusalem, our minds turn to Jerusalem of today. Jeru*salem*, which translates as 'the city of peace', but is in so many ways a city of intense conflict. A harsh military occupation imposed on the Palestinian people, illegal land confiscation by Israel for settlement expansion, house demolitions, suicide bombs by Palestinian extremists. Jesus, two thousand years ago, wept over Jerusalem, saying, 'If only you knew what made for peace.' Yet how much have we learned since? How much should we weep at the folly of humankind with its brutality, its desire to dominate, its exclusion of others?

With the suicide bombs in Jerusalem and the blowing up of the bombers' family homes in retribution, just what is achieved? An eye for an eye, the way of revenge, means that we will all end up blind. Since the bombings in Jerusalem and the siege of Palestinian cities like Jenin, Ramallah and Bethlehem, new occurrences of violence have developed. A little boy, Tabarak, who suffered from cerebral palsy, died last Easter, as the ambulance was unable to make it through the military checkpoints to his West Bank village in time. Pain and tragedy do not balance out on both sides like an equation. Pain and tragedy are borne by the whole human family. Tabarak's mother is known to have said, 'I don't want revenge, it won't bring me back my son or those who were lost in the suicide bomb. For the sake of all who have lost their lives, don't just talk peace, *do* peace.'

What do we do with the power we have – to hurt or to heal, to build or to destroy? It is only when peace founded on justice, acceptable to all, is *done* that Jerusalem will truly live up to its name – city of peace. It is only when there is peace that true justice and security can begin for the Palestinians and Israelis, only when we recognise God in every human being that we learn not to be afraid but to be forgiven and to forgive.

Pray not for Arab or Jew,
for Palestinian or Israeli
but pray rather for ourselves
that we may not divide them in our prayers
but keep them both together in our hearts.

(Based on a prayer by a Palestinian Christian)

Day 40

HOLY WEEK: RECONCILIATION THROUGH THE CROSS

DAVID PAIN

Palm Sunday: Hosanna!
John 12:9–16

They took palm branches and went out to meet him, shouting, 'Hosanna!' 'Blessed is he who comes in the name of the Lord!' 'Blessed is the King of Israel!' (John 12:13)

Have you ever been in the crowd arriving at a music concert or a major sporting event, jostling through the hordes at Twickenham, Wembley or Lord's? The ticket touts are having a field day – the carnival atmosphere reaches fever pitch – what will happen next? The atmosphere and excitement is not so far from the scene in Jerusalem – a great crowd gathering, the promise of a spectacle. Lazarus has been raised: what is the next trick this man from the outback can pull for the crowds?

Our eyes fall on this man on a donkey – a shocking sight when we expected to see the King of Israel. Our preconceptions are shaken to the core. Like the disciples, we are amazed that the King of Israel arrives on a donkey, vulnerable and powerless.

In times of war and conflict many of us light candles, perhaps outside in a vigil as a public witness or in our own homes as we take in the pain of the television news. A candle is by definition weak and vulnerable, yet it sheds light further than we would anticipate. A vulnerable yet defiant light.

When I was a teenager, the film *Gandhi* made a great impression on me: a great leader who wove his own clothes and cleaned his own house in a culture where such things would be considered below his status. His simple non-violent presence brought the might of the British Empire to its knees. Working in India soon after seeing the film, I was overawed by the size of the country – and here was one man who made such an impact there and for the way of peace all around the world.

The spirituality of peacemakers is subversive. Somehow the unexpected action overturns the power of force, absorbing the energy of violence and transforming it.

Our journey to the cross begins with this remarkable entry into Jerusalem and many questions: what kind of a man is this, what kind of a leader, what kind of peacemaker – what kind of Messiah? No triumphal band here, no military conquest, and yet we believe that the whole of creation is reconciled through the events that we recall this week.

Lord, I am constantly surprised by your ways. Your rule is so unlike any other power I experience, I pray for the imagination to take new steps this week as I journey with you to the cross.

Day 41

Truth and reconciliation
Isaiah 42:1–9

*Here is my servant, whom I uphold . . . he will bring justice
to the nations. He will not shout or cry out or raise his
voice in the streets. A bruised reed he will not break, and a
smouldering wick he will not snuff out. (Isaiah 42:1–3)*

Jesus, the suffering servant whom we follow to the cross, exposes
the reality of the world through a quiet persistent presence, like
a candle burning in defiance of the darkness. Isaiah describes how
as a light to the nations he will open the eyes of those that are
blind and bring the prisoners out from their dungeons. The light
of truth will bring justice. The covenant of the cross heralds the
dawn of the rule of justice, but the promise of the coming kingdom
is a challenge to all our relationships.

The witness of generations of Quakers has been that the means
of achieving peace will determine the ends. In 1693 William Penn
wrote: 'A good end cannot sanctify evil means; nor must we ever
do evil, that good may come of it . . . Let us then try what Love
would do . . . Force may subdue, but Love gains.'[3]

Many processes of reconciliation are built when people are able
to speak openly to each other of their experience, opening the eyes
of those who live in darkness to the reality of the suffering of
conflict and freeing the prisoners of history whose story is otherwise unheard. As we travel the journey to the cross, we call to
mind situations in which we know that the light of truth is needed
to bring peace and justice.

The Truth and Reconciliation process in South Africa was

certainly imperfect but an extraordinary achievement for a nation in coming to terms with the truth in order to build a lasting peace. During the hearings, I met with people who had both given evidence and attended sessions in which those who had lived in fear and hate for generations came face to face and started the process of change. Their sense of liberation was tangible.

In personal relationships it is all too easy to mistake a strained quiet for real peace. A relationship built on a commitment to speaking the hidden truth may be noisier at times, but ultimately the truth sets us free. A stronger peace is built if the journey through this pain is recognised as part of the essential nature of the relationship.

We pray for the opening of our eyes to the reality of the experience of others; help us to enter into their story in love. As we share the joys and sufferings of others, keep alive in us the still burning wick of the candle of peace.

Day 42

This is a people plundered and looted, all of them trapped in pits or hidden away in prisons. They have become plunder with no one to rescue them; they have been made loot, with no one to say, 'Send them back.' (Isaiah 42:22)

At home we have a garden shed to keep the lawnmower, garden tools and rather a lot of junk – it is a sturdy timber shed. Last year I met Teresa Maria and her five children. Their house is the size of our shed, but the walls are made of straw mats, the roof a plastic sheet. Teresa Maria is one of five thousand people living in a camp at Barro do Dande in Angola, one of four million in that country who have fled their homes and farms during forty years of war. In terms of health care, education and life expectancy, her five children are growing up in the worst country in the world. The victims of war are surely the people that peacemaking is all about – how will they be rescued? What does the reconciliation of the cross mean to these people?

Christian Aid exposes the scandal of poverty; one way it does this, in its publications and reports, is by naming the individuals whose lives are affected. The human face gives meaning to the statistics, but it is also at the heart of any Christian response to poverty, because we believe that each one of us is created, known and loved by God.

In Angola I also met Daniel Ntoni Nzinga, head of an ecumenical organisation that has brought the churches together in support of the peacebuilding process. In one conversation he said, with the pain of someone who knows the cost of conflict, 'When one suffers, no one is free.' At the cross we are united with the suffering of creation; and in the risen life we are part of a community that, while familiar with suffering, chooses the way of hope.

In Barro do Dande, Christian Aid's partner Action for Rural Development and the Environment works with people like Teresa Maria to build peace. Through asserting their human rights and the power of the community working together, people are discovering new resources in the face of great suffering.

The way of Jesus, the way of peace, is the calling to be fully alive; the reconciliation of the cross is not an acceptance of suffering, but its transformation. At the cross the rules of suffering are rewritten.

Lord, reading the newspaper today I stand with the victims of war whose names are dear to you. In the midst of their pain, which I share, I pray for the vision to know the ways in which I can play my part in building communities that will transform their suffering into hope.

Day 43

Streams on the dry ground
Isaiah 44:1–8

I will pour water on the thirsty land, and streams on the dry ground . . . Do not tremble, do not be afraid . . . Is there any God besides me? No, there is no other Rock. (Isaiah 44:3, 8)

Walking long distances in the heat of the day is never a good idea. For a tourist the wait for a cool drink can seem a test of endurance, yet for many the preservation of scarce water resources is a daily challenge. Whether we have experienced a desperate thirst ourselves or seen the experience of others in images on our television, we can pause for a moment to feel the thirst that is literally a matter of life and death. In the midst of conflict, the images of a parched land are a vivid metaphor of our desperate search for the hope-giving living waters of God.

Our hope for reconciliation through the cross is founded on our experience of the nature of the God whom we find in these dry places. Isaiah tells us that the promise of God's presence is like water poured on a thirsty land.

Liberation theologians have spoken of the need for the suffering Church to drink from its own wells of spirituality – to discover for itself the depth of life from within its own experience. Quakers speak of our experience of God being recognising the light within ourselves and in others. Like the disciples on the road to Emmaus, we may be surprised by the places in which we find God.

The vast expanses of desert in southern Africa, parched from the long drought, burst into colour as the flowers of spring appear seemingly from nowhere – the desert blooms! Places that we know to be dry and without hope bloom with possibilities and the God-given spirit of life. On our journey to the cross, the order of things is overturned by the way in which Jesus lived and died and the experience of the risen life that sustains his followers.

The choice to live a hope-filled risen life has often to be made in spite of the facts around us, in the face of the continuation of violence that marks all human society and is deep within ourselves. In the face of continued war and conflict we choose to hope, live and work for peace in our home, communities and nations because of the nature of God shown to us on the cross and in the risen life of Jesus.

> *Lord, I pray for your life-giving water in the parched land of conflict. I pray for the vision to tap into the waters of hope which run deep within me and those who travel with me on the way of the cross.*

Day 44

MAUNDY THURSDAY

ROWAN WILLIAMS

Defenceless love
Isaiah 49:1–7

I am honoured in the eyes of the Lord and my
God has been my strength. (Isaiah 49:5)

The servant of God calls to distant lands and peoples to say that God has given him the task of restoring both Israel and the nations to peace with God. The monarchs of distant countries will acknowledge his authority. Why? What makes his authority recognisable in a way that crosses the boundaries of culture and language like this?

The servant of God is someone who accepts defeat not in weakness, not in resentment, but in the conviction that only in accepting it can he break down the barriers between nations. By not pretending to strength, invulnerability, he is able to speak in a way that can be understood, to act in a way that makes a difference. The greatest barriers between individuals and communities arise when one party claims to be beyond failure and wounds; the deepest shared human experience is the experience of loss. God's servant cries out in lament for loss and failure, and so – miraculously as it seems – wins the hearing, even the obedience, of the kings of the nations.

The greater the appearance of invulnerability, the greater the barrier. So, too, the greater the appearance of invulnerability, the more shattering and transforming the letting-go of the apparent advantage. God, who is thought to be infinitely beyond wounds and loss, works here through a servant who offers his vulnerability to God so as to build healing and peace.

Our world lives by the great lie that invulnerability is possible and that it is the foundation of success and survival. The truth is that it is the worst and most destructive fantasy that can imprison human beings. From a 'Star Wars' defence shield to a protective trade policy to a habit of coldness and unforgivingness in inter-personal life, the same principle is at work: what takes first place is my safety. And the more that dominates, the deeper the gulf between me or us and the other becomes.

Jesus speaks at the level of what we most basically share – the knowledge that we cannot live without loss and cannot think without thinking of death. He is free from pretence. He is free to call to the ends of the earth and say: I am speaking your language, human language; I have said no to the fictions of safety, and I have given myself over in defenceless love to God and to the world. And this is the light that all can recognise.

Jesus, teach us to face our mortality without panic. Help us to communicate with one another from our wounds, our fears and our failures. May we recognise you as you come to us in those with no defences, and so learn to let down our own that we meet as needy, mortal beings, and in this meeting find true compassion for each other.

Day 45

GOOD FRIDAY

Where God chooses to be
Isaiah 52:13–53:3

He was despised, and we esteemed him not.
(Isaiah 53:3)

People who suffer often lose their human dignity. Suffering isn't necessarily noble; it can be degrading. It can make it harder to see in the sufferer a real humanity. We like to think that we would always notice offences against human dignity, always be moved by compassion. But the painful truth is that the worst suffering is that which makes people invisible, so that we don't see their outraged and insulted humanity, don't see the terrible offence to God's glory in acts of oppression and terror.

So here is God's servant, disfigured by torture to the extent that you wouldn't think he was really human. People ignore him; they walk past. They have got used to suffering – to the photographs of starving children, the statistics of death, the appeals of the charities. It has all become routine, and something in us says that we needn't really notice or bother.

But on Good Friday, God says: degraded, invisible suffering is where I am. Crucifixion was 'a death reserved for slaves', in the words of W.H. Auden's poem, and so in a very special sense a death for those who were invisible, without voice or rights. And (says God) when you have learned how to turn your eyes to the full reality of a humanity whose face and form are so obliterated or distorted by suffering, you have begun to learn how to turn your eyes to me. You have begun to honour the divine image that can't be destroyed.

Turn to him: this is where God has chosen to be, in that dimension of human life that seems least human, least meaningful. God shows what it is to *be* God by demonstrating the divine freedom to be wherever divine love is directed. God's presence depends on no sort of human success or human plausibility. Our love and admiration, which depends so much on success, beauty and credibility, has to be judged and changed and educated by God's love which sets no conditions and knows no place where it cannot live and act.

Jesus, may we never lose the freedom to recognise humanity, however oppressed, silenced, forgotten by the majority. Remind us daily of where you choose to be in your divine compassion; and make us boundlessly grateful that your love has the power to overstep all frontiers and limitations, to be with us wherever we are – in pain and in joy, in triumph and in loss, in life and in death.

Day 46

HOLY SATURDAY

Taking his place with the forgotten

Isaiah 53:4–12

He was assigned a grave with the wicked . . . though
he had done no violence. (Isaiah 53:9)

God's servant is given a burial place with 'the scum of the earth'. He is silenced by not even having a memorial; he belongs with the anonymous victims throughout history who have no one to mourn them, those whose bodies have vanished in mass graves. He takes his place with the forgotten – so that the cause and the need of the forgotten may become his cause, so that his voice may be their voice.

In this way the love of God moves in to supply the deficiencies of human love and human attention. The need for God's child, God's servant, to suffer in degradation and agony is that our love fails. So the servant's suffering arises from our collective failure, our common guilt. He is wounded because of our transgressions. Not simply that he takes the punishment due to us, but that our blindness and self-protectiveness is the root of his suffering. Because we cannot build bridges into the suffering of others, God's love must do it; and God's love can do it only by sharing that suffering.

So it is that this suffering is reconciling. It is God acting to *include* those who are shut out of the 'ordinary' round of human life – including even the dead in the scope and purpose of divine life. If as Christians we open ourselves up to receive what God gives in the death and resurrection of Jesus, we are taken into a great movement of embrace; we cannot regard the movement into the heart of the experience of the lost and humiliated as any kind of optional extra for us, because it is just this movement that God has swept us into. It is the movement into pain, into death, even into hell, into the place of no meanings and no hopes. We must go there with God, in Jesus. Our deficiencies, our fear and attempts to run away, no longer matter if we are truly ready to receive what God gives. It is our own absolution and reconciliation at the same time as it is our empowerment for the ministry of reconciliation.

Jesus, thank you for doing what I cannot do, for making the peace I cannot make, and leading me to the places where I cannot go in my own strength. You have taken me with you to the heart of human need; and you have taken me to the heart of God. In the midst of the darkness of need, you kindle the light of God's everlasting and victorious love. Keep me faithful to the light of that love.

Day 47

EASTER SUNDAY
The challenge of peace
John 20:19–23

Jesus said, 'Peace be with you! As the Father has sent me,
I am sending you.' (John 20:21)

This is the first time in the Gospels that we hear Jesus saying, 'Peace be with you.' It's as if he can only finally proclaim peace on the far side of the cross. We have seen the cost of reconciliation, of the crossing over to the side of the lost and forgotten; so now when we hear the word 'peace' we should also hear a challenge to ourselves. Jesus has made our peace, Jesus has made God's peace with those the world ignores; and that peace has been won by an act of identification that casts aside safety, private interest, tribal self-concerns.

If we are interested in peace in any other sense than our individual or group security (never mind the cost to others), we have to ask how we undermine the passion in us for such security. We have to learn some skills of discernment in human behaviour. Like the apostles, we have to distinguish through the Holy Spirit's power between behaviour that can be forgiven – because people open themselves up to new perspectives and face the truth about their fear and selfishness – and behaviour that has to be confronted, 'retained' until people acknowledge its destructive character.

Think of countries in the aftermath of civil war, genocidal violence, decades of injustice – Rwanda, South Africa, the Balkans. What brings peace? Sometimes people are so deeply set free by God's grace that they can respond when others acknowledge their guilt and can begin to build a new relationship. They are not imprisoned by being forever victims. But this seldom comes without the stage of 'retaining' sin or offence, waiting for it to be acknowledged by the offender, patiently holding up the truth to them. This already shows a willingness not to run away and ignore the call to make peace. But it also means that some sufferers are given the freedom to step across to the side of those who made them suffer – to confront and to heal. There are so many heart-rending stories from the South African Truth and Reconciliation Commission – not all with happy endings, by any means. But some of the stories do show the miracle of resurrection forgiveness – the wounds turned to healing.

No healing without cost. No healing without truth. But when the price is paid and the truth is told, there is healing at a depth we can barely imagine – the life of a new creation.

Jesus, give us courage to face the ways we have hurt or forgotten others; courage to face the hurt we ourselves have suffered; courage to face those who have made us suffer. Let us not make forgiveness cheap; but give us strength to believe in it and to let our lives be shaken and renewed by it – by your forgiveness of us and by your call to us to forgive in the liberty of your Spirit, the first gift of the resurrection life.

Notes

1   A. Boesak, *Walking on Thorns* (1984), Geneva: World Council of Churches.
2   W. Brueggemann, *Isaiah 1–39* (1998), Louisville, Kentucky: Westminster John Knox Press, p. 198.
3   *Quaker Faith and Practice*, 24.03.